What is an Ecosystem

Home Sweet Home

Producers

Herbivores

carnivores

Decomposers

Types of Ecosystems

Ocean Food Chain

Food chains in different ecosystems

Imagine a place where everything is connected, where plants, animals, and even tiny creatures work together to create a magical balance. This incredible place is called an ecosystem!

What is an Ecosystem?

An ecosystem is like a big, bustling community where living things, like plants and animals, and non-living things, like soil, water, and sunlight, all come together and interact in amazing ways. It's like a giant puzzle, with each piece fitting perfectly to keep everything in harmony.

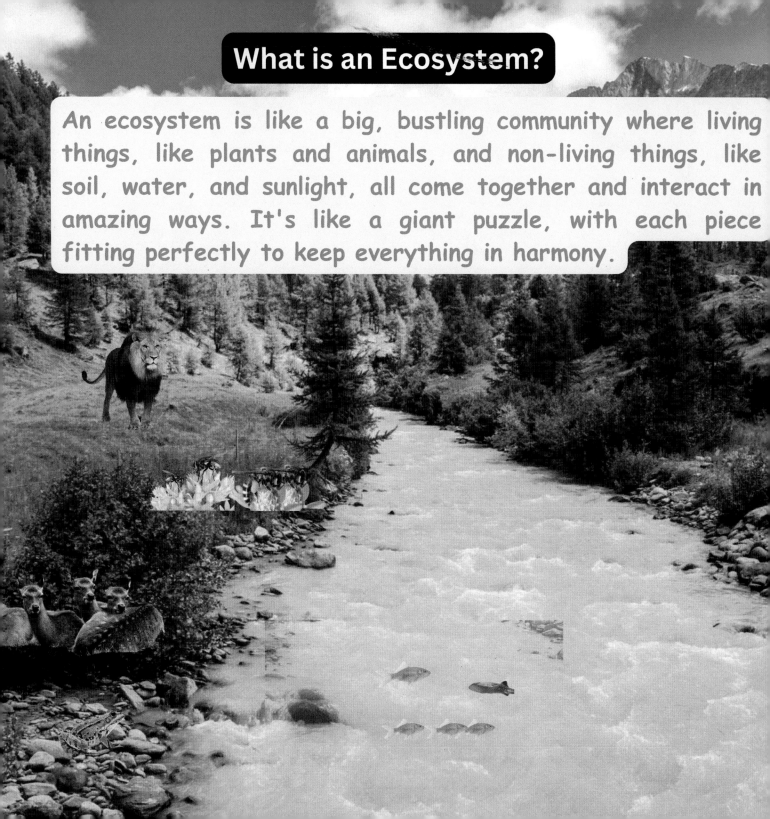

Home Sweet Home

Ecosystems can be found all around us, from the towering trees of the forest to the sandy shores of the beach, and even in your very own backyard! Each ecosystem has its own special features and unique inhabitants, making every place on Earth special and important.

producers

In an ecosystem, there are many different types of creatures called organisms. Some, like plants, make their own food using sunlight, water, and air. We call these clever plants "producers" because they produce their own food.

producers   **Because they produce their own food.**

Herbivores

Then, there are animals that eat plants. We call them "herbivores."

They munch on tasty leaves, stems, and fruits to fuel their busy lives.

carnivores

But wait, there's more! There are also animals that eat other animals. These hungry creatures are called "carnivores." They have sharp teeth and strong jaws to catch and eat their prey.

cheetah

fox

Tiger

Lion

Leopord

Decomposers

And let's not forget about the helpful decomposers! These tiny organisms, like bacteria and fungi, work hard to break down dead plants and animals, turning them into nutrients that plants can use to grow big and strong.

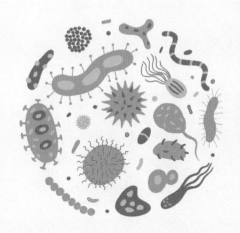
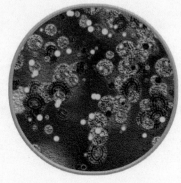

producers

Herbivores

carnivores

Decomposers

Types of Ecosystems

Forests: Dense collections of trees and plants, forests are home to a wide variety of animals, including deer, bears, birds, and insects. They play a crucial role in oxygen production and carbon dioxide absorption.

Grasslands: Vast expanses of grasses and herbs, grasslands are inhabited by grazing animals like buffalo, zebras, and antelope, as well as predators like lions and wolves. They are essential for agriculture and provide habitats for many species.

Deserts: Dry and arid regions with limited vegetation, deserts are inhabited by specialized plants and animals adapted to extreme conditions, such as cacti, camels, and scorpions. Water conservation and temperature regulation are key adaptations for survival.

Oceans: Massive bodies of saltwater covering most of Earth's surface, oceans are teeming with diverse life, including fish, whales, sharks, and countless other marine organisms. Coral reefs, kelp forests, and deep-sea trenches are some of the unique habitats found within oceans.

Freshwater Habitats: Lakes, rivers, streams, and ponds make up freshwater ecosystems, supporting a variety of aquatic life such as fish, frogs, turtles, and aquatic plants. These habitats are vital sources of drinking water and provide important ecosystems services.

1. The Sun Light from the sun gives plants energy.

2. Tiny plants that use sunlight to make food.

6. Great White Shark This predator is a quick and powerful hunter. It eats the seal.

5. Seals or Sea Lions: Marine mammals that prey on smaller fish

4. Predatory Fish: Larger fish like tuna that eat smaller fish.

4. Small Fish: Fish like anchovies that eat krill..

3. small shrimp-like creatures that eat phytoplankton.

Ocean Food Chain

Phytoplankton: At the base of the ocean food chain are tiny organisms called phytoplankton. These microscopic plants float near the surface of the water and use sunlight to make their own food through photosynthesis.

Krill: Next in the food chain are krill, small shrimp-like creatures that feed on phytoplankton. They are an essential food source for many marine animals, including fish, whales, and seabirds.

Small Fish: Small fish, such as anchovies or herring, consume krill as part of their diet. They play a vital role in transferring energy from lower trophic levels to higher ones.

Predatory Fish: Larger predatory fish, like tuna or barracuda, feed on smaller fish. These carnivorous fish use their speed and sharp teeth to catch their prey.

Seals or Sea Lions: Seals and sea lions are examples of marine mammals that feed on smaller fish and other marine creatures. They hunt by diving underwater and using their agility to catch their prey.

Sharks: Apex predators like sharks are at the top of the ocean food chain. They have few natural predators and are known for their powerful jaws and keen hunting abilities. Sharks feed on a variety of marine animals, including fish, seals, and even other sharks.

Food Chains

Imagine a game of passing energy from one player to the next. This is how a food chain works in nature! Let's look at a simple example:

Grass: Our game starts with the grass, which is like the energy source. Grass uses sunlight to make food through a process called photosynthesis.

Grasshopper: Next, along comes a hungry grasshopper. It eats the grass to get the energy it needs to hop around and grow.

Frog: Now, a frog hops onto the scene. It sees the grasshopper and thinks, "Yum!" The frog catches and eats the grasshopper for dinner.

Snake: Slithering in, a snake spies the frog and thinks it would make a tasty snack. The snake grabs the frog and swallows it whole.

Hawk: Finally, a hawk swoops down from the sky, spotting the snake. With a quick dive, the hawk snatches the snake in its talons and carries it away to enjoy as its meal.

Food chains in different ecosystems

Arctic Tundra

Producer: Arctic Moss
Primary Consumer: Lemming
Secondary Consumer: Arctic Fox
Tertiary Consumer: Polar Bear

Savanna Grassland

Producer: **Grass**
Primary Consumer: **Antelope**
Secondary Consumer: **Lion**
Tertiary Consumer: **Hyena**

Temperate Deciduous Forest:

Producer: **Oak Tree**
Primary Consumer: **Caterpillar**
Secondary Consumer: **Blue Jay**
Tertiary Consumer: **Red Fox**

Coral Reef

Producer: Coral Polyps
Primary Consumer: Zooplankton
Secondary Consumer: Parrotfish
Tertiary Consumer: Reef Shark

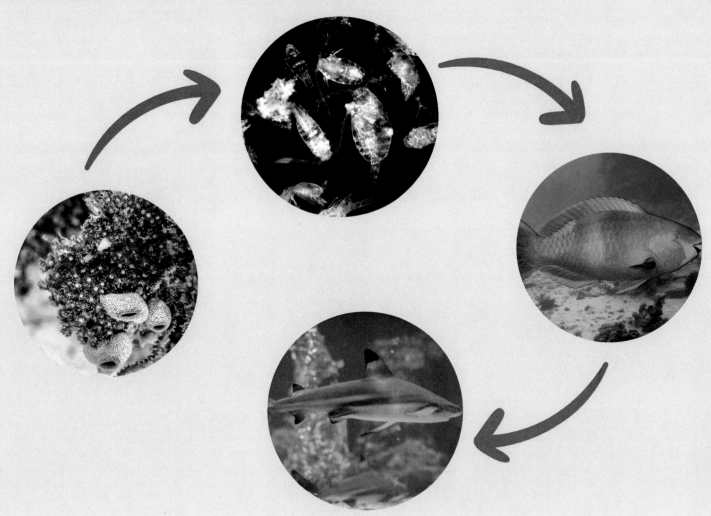

Freshwater Pond

Producer: Algae

Primary Consumer: Daphnia (Water Flea)

Secondary Consumer: Small Fish (like Minnows)

Tertiary Consumer: Large Fish (like Bass)

Deep Sea

Producer: **Phytoplankton**

*Primary Consumer: **Krill***

*Secondary Consumer: **Squid***

*Tertiary Consumer: **Sperm Whale***

Desert

Producer: Cactus

Primary Consumer: Desert Grasshopper

Secondary Consumer: Lizard

Tertiary Consumer: Coyote

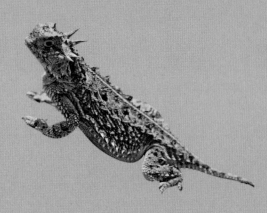

Salt Marsh

Producer: **Spartina Grass**
Primary Consumer: **Marsh Crab**
Secondary Consumer: **Fish (like Mullet)**
Tertiary Consumer: **Osprey**

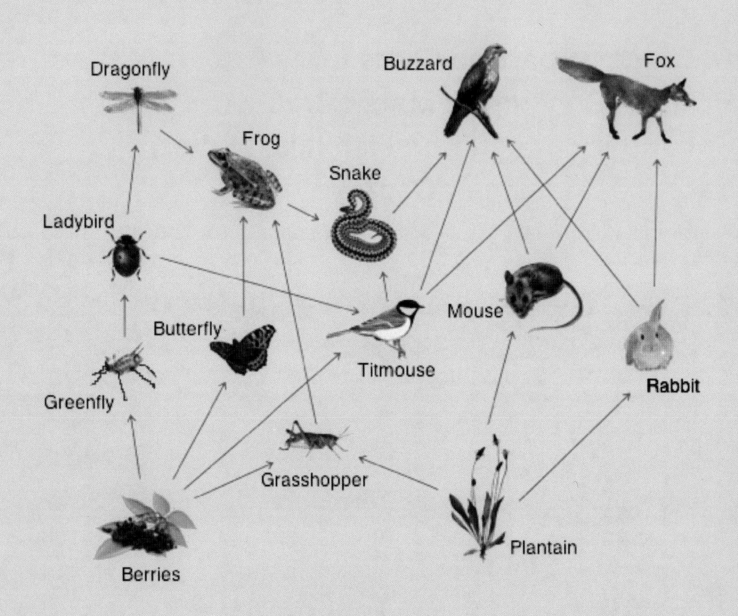

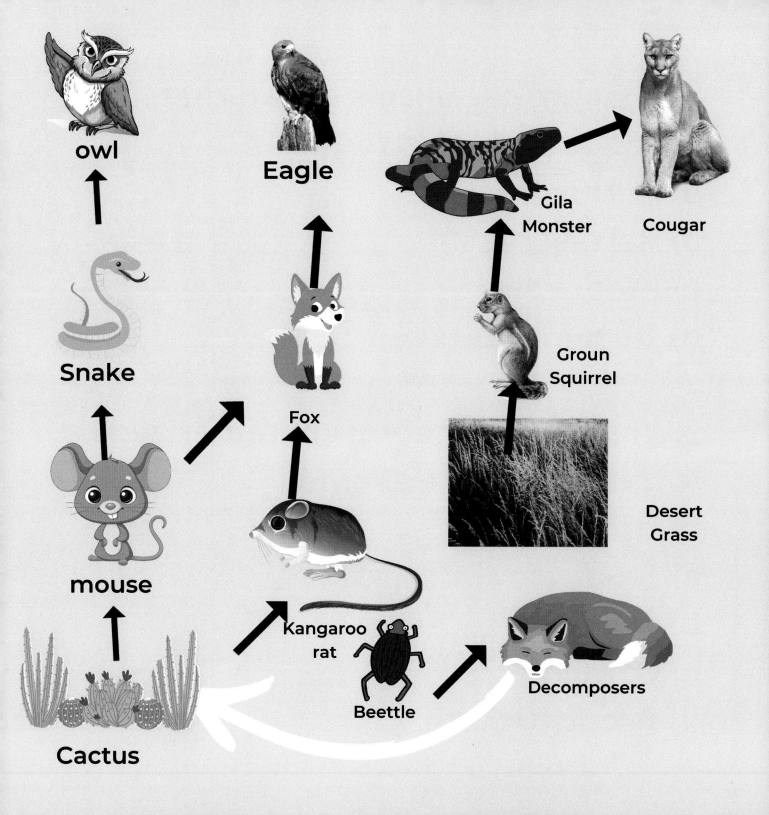

1.What are organisms called that produce their own food?
a) Herbivores
b) Carnivores
c) Producers
d) Decomposers

2.Which ecosystem is characterized by low rainfall and extreme temperatures?
a) Tropical rainforest
b) Desert
c) Coral reef
d) Arctic tundra

3.What are animals called that eat both plants and animals?
a) Herbivores
b) Carnivores
c) Omnivores
d) Decomposers

4.Which ecosystem is characterized by vast open areas dominated by grasses and scattered trees?
a) Tropical rainforest
b) Grassland
c) Tundra
d) Coral reef

5.What is the process by which plants use sunlight to make food?

a) Respiration

b) Decomposition

c) Photosynthesis

d) Predation

6.Where would you most likely find coral reefs?

a) Arctic Ocean

b) Atlantic Ocean

c) Indian Ocean

d) Mediterranean Sea

7.Which of the following is not a freshwater ecosystem?
a) River
b) Lake
c) Pond
d) Coral reef

8.What are animals called that feed on dead plants and animals?
a) Herbivores
b) Carnivores
c) Producers
d) Decomposers

9.Which ecosystem is characterized by cold temperatures and vast expanses of ice?

a) Rainforest
b) Grassland
c) Desert
d) Polar region

10.What is the primary source of energy for most ecosystems?

a) Soil
b) Air
c) Water
d) Sunlight

1. **c) Producers**
2. **b) Desert**
3. **c) Omnivores**
4. **b) Grassland**
5. **c) Photosynthesis**
6. **c) Indian Ocean**
7. **d) Coral reef**
8. **d) Decomposers**
9. **d) Polar region**
10. **d) Sunlight**

1. In an ecosystem, _____ are like nature's builders, capturing sunlight to make food through a process called _____.

2. _____ are animals that eat plants, also known as _____.

3. _____ are animals that eat other animals and are called _____.

4. _____ are tiny organisms that break down dead plants and animals, returning nutrients to the soil.

5. A _____ is a place where living things, like plants and animals, and non-living things, like soil and water, all come together and interact.

6.The Arctic Tundra is a cold and icy ecosystem with short summers and long winters, home to animals like polar bears, Arctic foxes, and _____.

7.Coral reefs are found in warm, shallow waters and are made up of tiny animals called _____.

8.Rainforests are _____ ecosystems found near the equator, home to a wide variety of plants and animals, including colorful birds, monkeys, and _____.

9.Grasslands, also known as prairies, are vast open areas dominated by _____ and scattered trees, supporting grazing animals like bison, antelope, and _____.

10.Freshwater ecosystems include _____ like rivers, lakes, and ponds, and provide habitats for aquatic life such as fish, frogs, and _____.

1. **producers, photosynthesis**
2. **Herbivores, plant-eaters**
3. **Carnivores, meat-eaters**
4. **Decomposers**
5. **ecosystem**
6. **caribou**
7. **coral polyps**
8. **tropical, jaguars**
9. **grass, zebras**
10. **bodies of water, ducks**